It's Catching

Head Lice

Angela Royston

H **www.heinemann.co.uk**
Visit our website to find out more information about **Heinemann Library** books.

To order:
☎ Phone 44 (0) 1865 888066
▤ Send a fax to 44 (0) 1865 314091
▢ Visit the Heinemann Bookshop at www.heinemann.co.uk to browse our catalogue and order online.

First published in Great Britain by Heinemann Library,
Halley Court, Jordan Hill, Oxford OX2 8EJ
a division of Reed Educational and Professional Publishing Ltd.
Heinemann is a registered trademark of Reed Educational & Professional Publishing Ltd.

OXFORD MELBOURNE AUCKLAND JOHANNESBURG BLANTYRE
GABORONE IBADAN PORTSMOUTH (NH) USA CHICAGO

Designed by David Oakley/Arnos Design
Originated by Dot Gradations
Printed in Hong Kong/China

ISBN 0 431 12853 7
05 04 03 02 01
10 9 8 7 6 5 4 3 2 1

British Library Cataloguing in Publication Data
Royston, Angela
  Head lice. – (It's catching)
  1. Pediculosis
  I. Title
  614.4'324

Acknowledgements
The Publishers would like to thank the following for permission to reproduce photographs:
Bubbles pp 5 (Ian West), 20 (Jennie Woodcock), 25 (Jennie Woodcock), 29 (Pauline Cutler), Corbis pp7 (Carl Purcell), 26 (Roger Ressmeyer), Gareth Boden pp18, 19, 21, Martin Soukias p22, NHPA p4, Powerstock (Zefa) p28, Robert Harding p10, Sally and Richard Greenhill p8, Science Photo Library pp6, 12 (Mark Clarke), 14 (Sinclair Stammers), 15 (J C Revy), 17 (David Scharf), 24 (Dr Chris Hale), Stone (Jerome Tisne) p9, Tony Stone pp11 (Bob Torrez), 16 (Tim Flach), 23 (Andy Sacks), Trevor Clifford pp13, 27.

Cover photograph reproduced with permission of Science Photo Library.

Every effort has been made to contact copyright holders of any material reproduced in this book. Any omissions will be rectified in subsequent printings if notice is given to the Publisher.

Any words appearing in bold, **like this**, are explained in the glossary.

Contents

What are head lice?

Head lice are small **insects** that live in human hair. This louse has been **magnified** so that you can see what it looks like. A real louse is only 2 or 3 millimetres long.

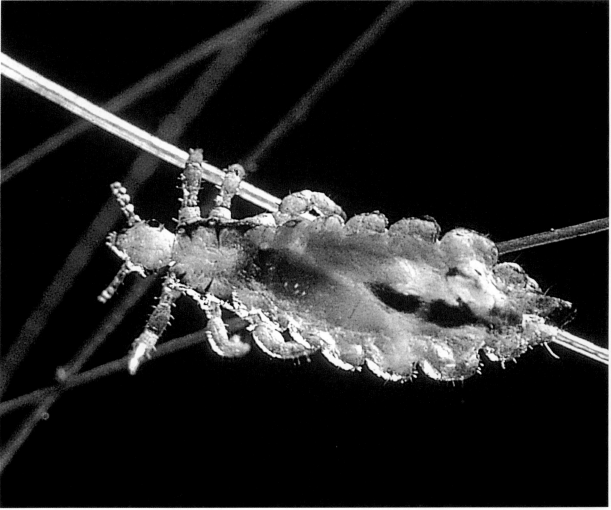

A louse is smaller than the tip of a match. It moves so fast through the hair that it can be very difficult to spot.

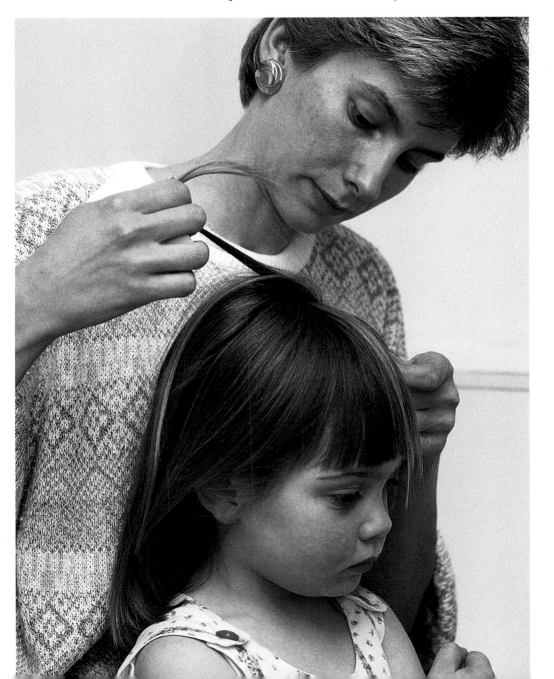

A healthy scalp

This is a **magnified** photo of a **scalp** – the layer of skin that covers your head. Hair grows longer and more thickly on the scalp than anywhere else on the body.

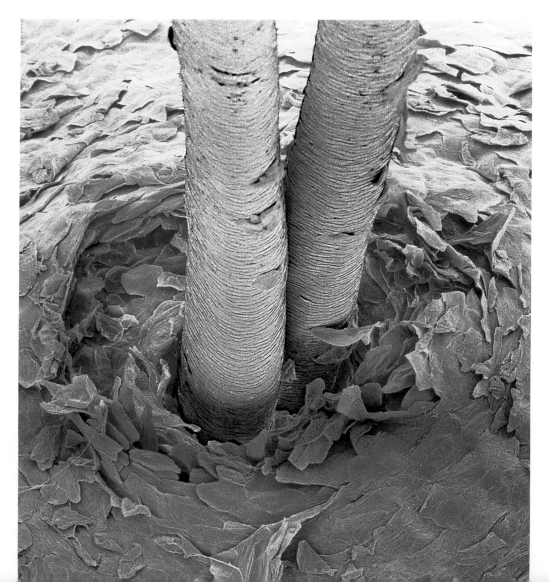

Hair protects your scalp from the sun's rays. It also helps to keep you warm. It stops heat in your body from escaping through your scalp.

Passing them on

Head lice pass very easily from one person's hair to another. Your head often touches the heads of your friends and classmates.

Your hair also touches the heads of the other people in your family. If one person has head lice, soon all their friends and family will have them, too!

Who gets head lice?

Anyone who has hair can get head lice! People with short hair can catch them just as easily as people with long hair.

If you have head lice, it does not mean your hair is dirty. Lice like a clean **scalp**. The most common age for catching lice is around six years.

First signs

The first thing a louse does when it crawls into your hair is bite your **scalp**. Some people begin to itch as soon as the louse bites them.

Other people do not itch until several weeks later. You cannot get rid of lice by washing your hair with ordinary **shampoo**.

What happens next

The louse lays many tiny eggs on the hair about a centimetre from the **scalp**. The eggs stick to the hair so hard, you cannot pull them off.

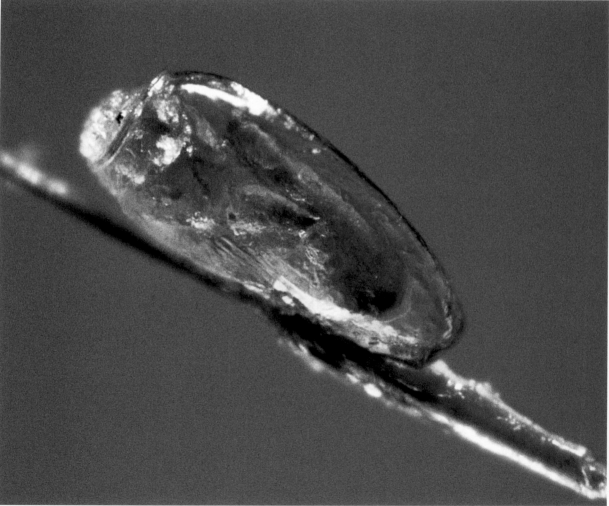

After about a week, a young louse **hatches** from the egg. The empty shell stays glued to the hair. It is called a **nit**.

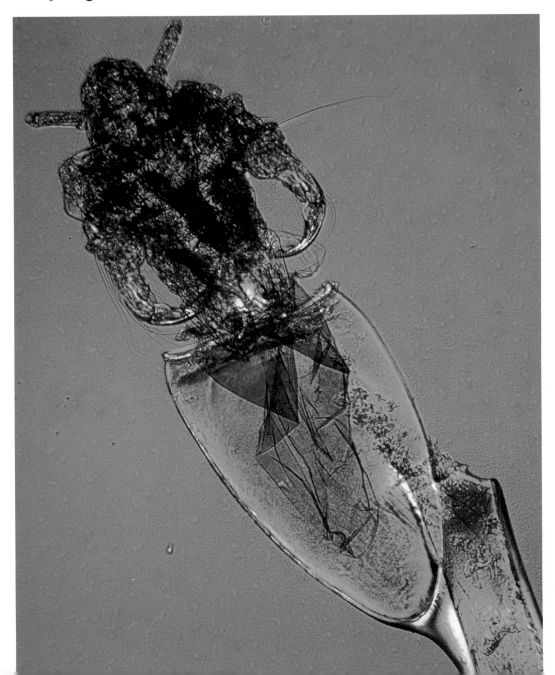

Many lice

The young lice feed by sucking blood from the **scalp**. They have special claws that grip the hair.

The young lice grow fast. They start to lay eggs themselves when they are only about ten days old. Soon the hair is full of lice!

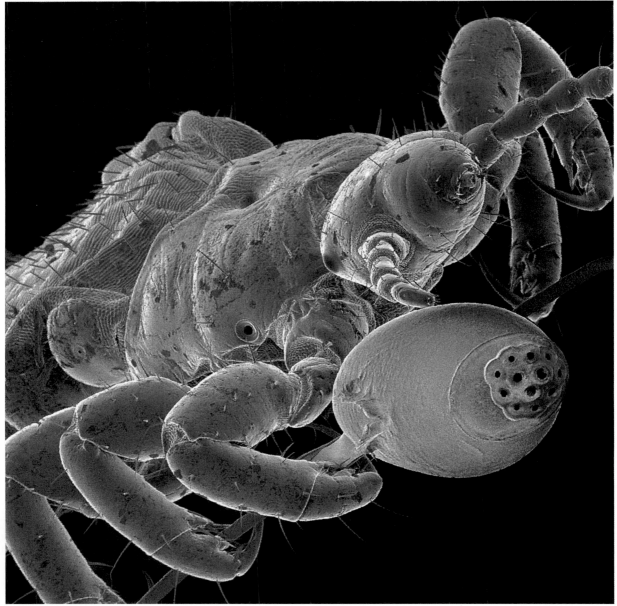

Getting rid of lice

Special **shampoos** contain strong **chemicals** that kill the lice. Sometimes though, these shampoos do not work because the lice get used to them.

Some people use a special **herbal** shampoo to kill the lice instead. Everyone in the family has to wash their hair at the same time.

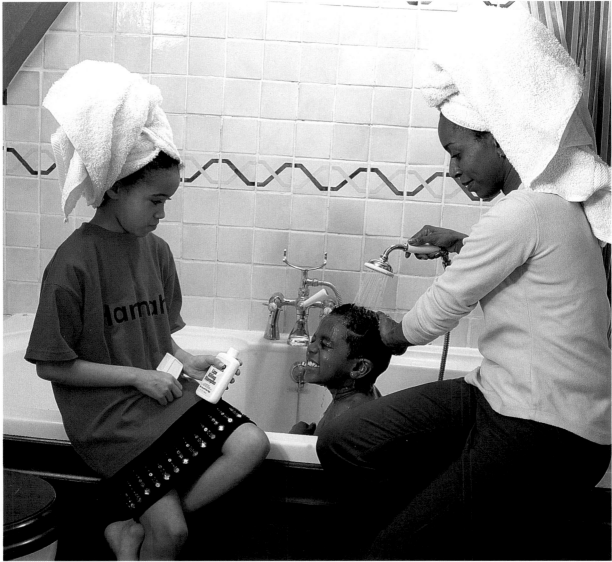

Combing out the lice

Nit combs have teeth that are very close together. When you have used the special **shampoo**, you can use a nit comb to comb out the dead lice and nits.

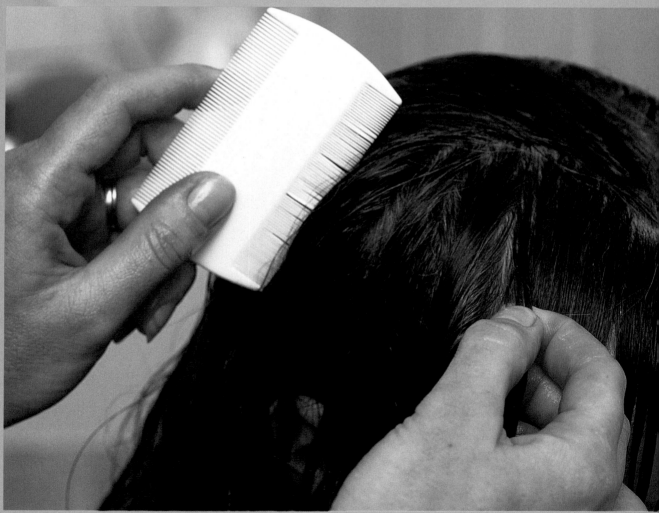

Another way to get rid of lice is to soak the hair in **olive oil** and leave it overnight. Then you can comb the lice out with a nit comb.

Bug-busting

Two weeks after **shampooing** or oiling your hair, you must do it again. This is to kill any lice that have **hatched** out since.

The best way to get rid of lice altogether
is for everyone in your class, or school, to
shampoo their heads on the same night.

On the lookout

The sooner you notice that you have lice, the sooner you can get rid of them. Check your hair regularly for **nits** like these.

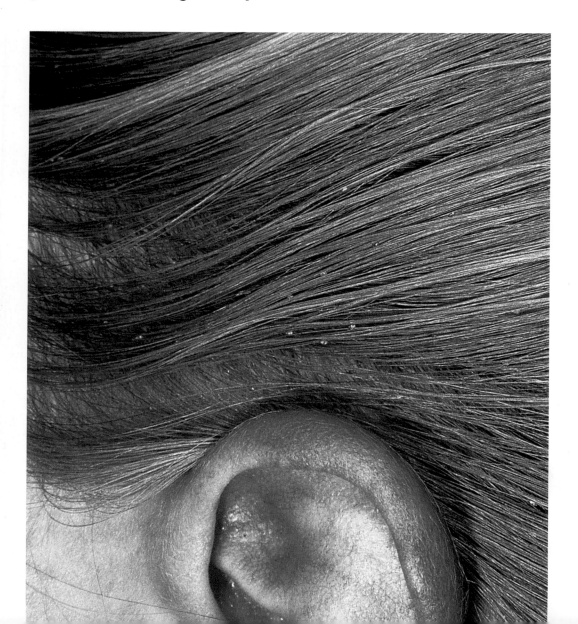

When you wash your hair, comb it with a nit comb and look for lice on the comb. Tell your parents and teacher if you find anything.

Healthy and well

You cannot stop lice getting into your hair – lice like clean hair just as much as you do. If you live a healthy life though, you will get fewer other illnesses.

Eat good food and take lots of exercise. Keep yourself clean, wash your hands before you eat and make sure you sleep well!

Think about it!

Maria says that **plaiting** her hair helps to stop her from getting head lice. Do you think that she is right or wrong?*

Sam has told his teacher that he has head lice. His friends won't play with him because they say he is dirty. Are they right?*

*Answers on page 30.

Answers

Page 28

Lice will crawl into any hair they come into contact with, so Maria can still catch head lice. Hair pulled close to the skull in plaits or a pony tail may be less likely to touch another person's hair though.

Page 29

Having head lice does not mean that you are dirty. In fact, head lice prefer clean hair. Sam must have caught them from someone else who had them. His friends are probably already infected, too. It is unkind not to play with him and it will not stop them getting head lice.

Stay healthy and safe!

1   Always tell an adult if you feel ill or think there is something wrong with you.
2   Never take any **medicine** or use any ointment or lotion unless it is given to you by an adult you trust.
3   Remember, the best way to stay healthy and safe is to eat good food, to drink plenty of water, to keep clean and to wear the correct clothes.

Glossary

chemicals   substances that things are made of

hatch   when an animal breaks out of the egg in which it has formed

herbal   made from plants

insects   small creatures that have six legs

magnified   made bigger so that you can see it more clearly

medicine   substance used to treat or prevent an illness

nit   empty shell that a louse leaves behind when it has hatched

olive oil   thick liquid made by squeezing the fruits of the olive tree

plaiting   criss-crossing three strands of hair together to form a braid

scalp   skin that covers your head and from which your hair grows

shampoo   special kind of liquid soap used to wash your hair

Index

Titles in the *It's Catching* series include:

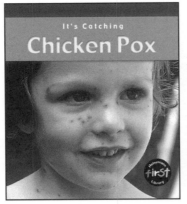

Hardback   0 431 12850 2

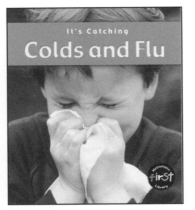

Hardback   0 431 12851 0

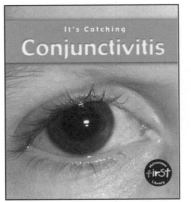

Hardback   0 431 12852 9

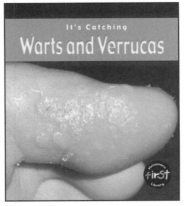

Hardback   0 431 12853 7

Hardback   0 431 12854 5

Find out about the other titles in this series on our website www.heinemann.co.uk/library